Next up for *The Prince of Tennis* is a live-action film*. It's not like we're jumping on the manga-based movie trend: we'd planned on doing the film even before we did the anime movie. We've been working on it behind closed doors for about two years now, so the quality should be top-notch. I make a tiny appearance in it: be on the lookout for me!

— Takeshi Konomi, 2005

*The film, titled *The Prince of Tennis,* was released in Japan in 2006.—Ed.

About Takeshi Konomi

Takeshi Konomi exploded onto the manga scene with the incredible **THE PRINCE OF TENNIS**. His refined art style and sleek character designs proved popular with **Weekly Shonen Jump** readers, and **THE PRINCE OF TENNIS** became the number one sports manga in Japan almost overnight. Its cast of fascinating male tennis players attracted legions of female readers even though it was originally intended to be a boys' comic. The manga continues to be a success in Japan and has inspired a hit anime series, as well as several video games and mountains of merchandise.

THE PRINCE OF TENNIS
VOL. 32
The SHONEN JUMP Manga Edition

STORY AND ART BY
TAKESHI KONOMI

Translation/Joe Yamazaki
Touch-up Art & Lettering/Vanessa Satone
Design/Sam Elzway
Editor/Leyla Aker

VP, Production/Alvin Lu
VP, Publishing Licensing/Rika Inouye
VP, Sales & Product Marketing/Gonzalo Ferreyra
VP, Creative/Linda Espinosa
Publisher/Hyoe Narita

Printed in the U.S.A.

Published by VIZ Media, LLC
P.O. Box 77010
San Francisco, CA 94107

SHONEN JUMP Manga Edition
10 9 8 7 6 5 4 3 2 1
First printing, July 2009

SHONEN JUMP Manga

VOL. 32

Two of a Cunning Kind

Story & Art by

Takeshi Konomi

ENNIS CLUB

• TAKASHI KAWAMURA • KUNIMITSU TEZUKA • SHUICHIRO OISHI • RYOMA ECHIZEN •

STORY & CHARACTERS

Seishun Academy student Ryoma Echizen is a tennis prodigy, with wins in four consecutive U.S. Junior Tennis Tournaments under his belt. He became a starter as a 7th grader and led his team to the District Preliminaries! Despite a few mishaps, Seishun won the District Prelims and the City Tournament, and earned a ticket to the Kanto Tournament. The team came away victorious from its first-round matches, but captain Kunimitsu injured his shoulder and went to Kyushu for treatment. Despite losing Kunimitsu and assistant captain Shuichiro to injury, Seishun pulled together as a team, winning the Kanto Tournament and earning a slot at the Nationals!

With Kunimitsu recovered and back on the team, Seishun enter the Nationals with their strongest line-up and defeat Okinawa's Higa Junior High in the opening round to advance to the semifinals. Their next opponent is Hyotei, who are eager to avenge their loss to Seishun in the Kanto Tournament. The first match is No. 3 Singles, with Momo facing Yushi Oshitari. Will the cunning techniques Momo honed prior to the tournament help him against Hyotei's resident genius?!

SEIGAKU T

• KAORU KAIDO • TAKESHI MOMOSHIRO • SADAHARU INUI • EIJI KIKUMARU • SHUSUKE FUJI •

TARO SAKAKI
HYOTEI ACADEMY TENNIS COACH

SUMIRE RYUZAKI
SEISHUN ACADEMY TENNIS COACH

WAKASHI HIYOSHI
HYOTEI ACADEMY

GAKUTO MUKAHI
HYOTEI ACADEMY

KEIGO ATOB
HYOTEI ACADEMY

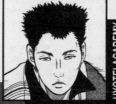

MUNEHIRO KABAJI
HYOTEI ACADEMY

YUSHI OSHITARI
HYOTEI ACADEMY

CONTENTS

Vol. 32
Two of a Cunning Kind

GENIUS 274: TWO OF A CUNNING KIND

SEISHUN IS NO LONGER THE SAME TEAM WE PLAYED AGAINST IN THE KANTO TOURNAMENT.
BUT EVEN IF WE ARE EQUALLY MATCHED IN STRENGTH NOW, HYOTEI WILL EMERGE VICTORIOUS.
YUSHI.
IT'S YOUR TURN.
FWP
HYOTEI ACADEMY TENNIS COACH TARO SAKAKI (AGE 43)

THE SEISHUN (TOKYO) VS. HYOTEI (TOKYO) MATCH WILL NOW BEGIN. THE FIRST MATCH IS NO. 3 SINGLES. PLAYERS, PLEASE PROCEED TO THE COURT.
ALL RIGHT! I WANNA HEAR YOU GUYS!!

Aw, c'mon!

MOMO, I CAN'T REACH IT IF YOU THROW IT LIKE—

DSH

IT'LL BE FINE.

SSH...

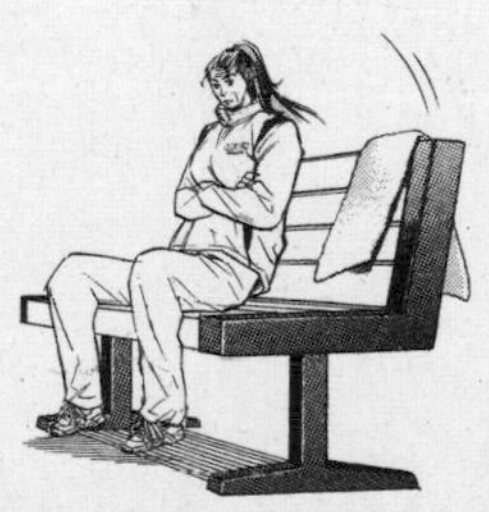

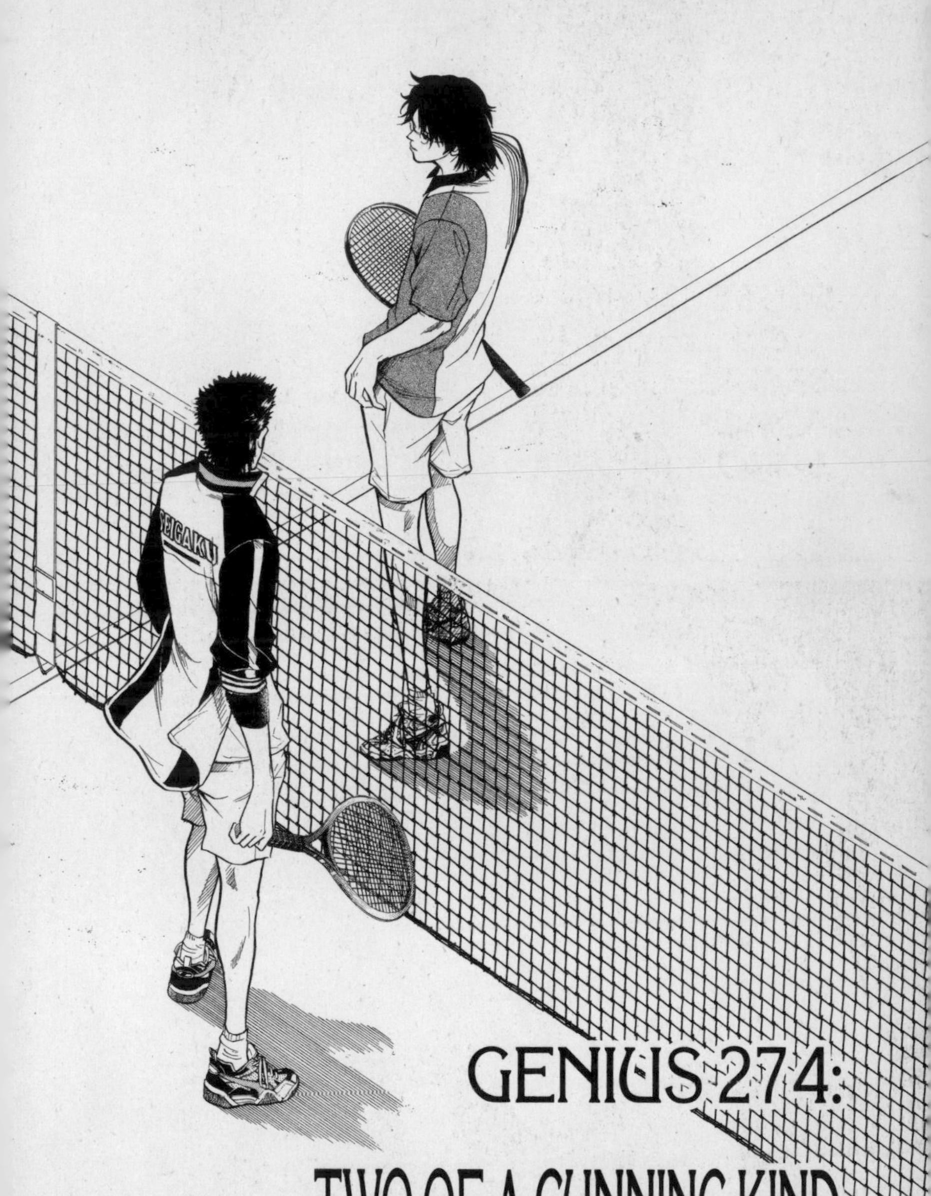

GENIUS 274: TWO OF A CUNNING KIND

SO IT'S YOU AGAIN... MOMO-SHIRO.
HEY, YOUR-SELF.

ONE-SET MATCH!

HYO-TEI!! HYO-TEI!!

SEISHUN'S MOMO-SHIRO TO SERVE!

SEI-SHUN! SEI-SHUN!
SEI-SHUN! SEI-SHUN !!
HYOTEI!! HYOTEI!!

IT'S MY FIRST GAME IN A WHILE. I'M SO HAPPY IT'S GIVING ME THE SHIVERS.

JUST SHUT UP AND SERVE.
OH, SORRY.

THEN I'LL GET THIS GAME STARTED !!
SEIGAKU
IT'S MOMO'S BULLET SERVE!

HE'S GAINED MORE ...

...POWER THAN I THOUGHT.

THAT WAS INTEN- TIONAL.
WAA
15- LOVE!
AN ACE RIGHT OFF THE BAT!

YOU SHOULD PICK UP THAT PEBBLE BY YOUR FEET...
YUSHI.
HE SAW SOME-THING THIS TINY FROM THERE?
WAAAA
VMM
VSH

I SEE NOW.
HE'S USING ONLY ABOUT 70% OF HIS POWER.
AND HE CHANGED HIS PLAY-STYLE TO A MORE CONTROL-ORIENTED ONE.
HOW-EVER ...
...THAT TYPE OF PLAYER IS EASIER TO BRING DOWN.
TMP...
A DROP SHOT ?!

!

MOMO KNEW IT WAS COMING!!

NICE, MOMO!!

TH- THIS TIME IT'S A LOB...
HUAAAA!
HAH!!

LIKE I SAID, NOT ENOUGH...
MORE ACTION! I NEED MORE ACTION!!
THAT'S RIGHT.
THE MOMO I KNOW WILL GET TO THAT BALL.
IT'S NO GOOD. MOMO'S LOST HIS PACE!

WAIT, HE'S GOT IT?! INCRED-IBLE!
BUT...
...IT'S STILL NOT ENOUGH.

NO ...
IT'LL BE FINE.

BOOM.

テニスの王子様
THE
PRINCE
OF
TENNIS

GENIUS 275: AN UNREADABLE OPPONENT
Hyuuu...
NO PROBLEM.
IT'LL BE FINE.

HE TOOK THE DIREC- TION OF THE WIND INTO ACCOUNT ...
GENIUS 275:
AN UNREADABLE OPPONENT

Boom
GAME, MOMO-SHIRO! 3 GAMES TO LOVE

THAT WAS AWE-SOME, MOMO! YOU'RE MY HERO!
WA A—A
MOMO MADE A BREAK-THROUGH WHILE TRAINING IN THE MOUNTAINS.

WH-
WHAT'S
GOING
ON?!
WAAAAA
YUSHI'S
SETTING
THE PACE
OF THE
GAME,
BUT...

...MOMO'S CUNNING.

SEIGAKU

HIS SENSES ARE SO HIGHLY SHARPENED RIGHT NOW THAT...
...HE CAN FEEL THE DIRECTION OF THE WIND AND HEAR THE SOUNDS THE BALL MAKES.
HE CAN DETECT YUSHI'S SMALLEST GESTURES: HIS BREATH, HIS EYE MOVEMENT... EVEN HIS THOUGHTS.

FOR REAL? THAT'S SO COOL!

HE HASN'T PLAYED THROUGH A TON OF CHALLENGES FOR NOTHING.

SHPA
VISH
THIS ONE'S MINE.
WHAT ?!
EVEN THE POSI- TION OF THE SUN?!

WSH
H-HE LOST SIGHT OF THE BALL!
ALL I NEED ...
...IS THE SHADOW.
WWWWWM

HE'S HIDING THE BALL'S SHADOW WITH HIS OWN.

HE'S CALMLY OBSERVING HIS SURROUND-INGS...
...THE SITUATION...
...EVEN MY THOUGHTS.
GAME, MOMO-SHIRO! 4 GAMES TO LOVE!
YES! YES! GO, MOMO!
WAAAAA
MOMO...
SO YOU FINALLY REALIZED WHAT YOUR GREATEST WEAPON IS.

MOMO! MOMO!
MOMO! MOMO!
MOMO! MOMO!
SEIGAKU

TEAM
S3
D
SEISHUN ACADEMY (TOKYO)
4
HYOTEI ACADEMY (TOKYO)
0
MOMO! MOMO!
GO, MOMO! SWEEP! SWEEP!
SHOW HIM THAT SHOT OF YOURS!
WAAAA
MOMO! MOMO!
YOU GOT IT.

TUD

TUD

I CAN'T READ HIM...

YOU'RE NO MATCH FOR ME, MOMO-SHIRO.

テニスの王子様
THE PRINCE OF TENNIS

GENIUS 276: SOURCE OF STRENGTH

SEIGAKU

GENIUS 276:
SOURCE OF STRENGTH

THE 3RD CHARACTER POPULARITY POLL RESULTS!!

1ST  **RYOMA ECHIZEN (13,578 VOTES)**
"Huh. I'm not really into this sort of stuff, so [whack]... Uh, thanks."

2ND  **SHUSUKE FUJI (12,459 VOTES)**
"It's so nice of everyone to always vote me so high. Thanks so much."

3RD  **KEIGO ATOBE (9,782 VOTES)**
"Me, finish third? This poll was obviously rigged."

4TH  **KUNIMITSU TEZUKA (9,578 VOTES)**
"I'd like to thank everybody who voted for— Hm? ... That's all!"

5TH  **YUSHI OSHITARI (7,413 VOTES)**
"Thanks, I really appreciate it. Wanna go get some takoyaki soon?"

6TH  **SADAHARU INUI (5,989 VOTES)**
"Th-There's no logic to this... [tears of joy]."

7TH  **AKAYA KIRIHARA (5,023 VOTES)**
"I'm close to the top now [smirk]. Next time I'll crush them all. ♡"

... 'COURSE IT'LL BE...

... MORE FUN THIS WAY.

HUAAA!!
MOMO-SHIRO...
I APPLAUD YOU FOR SHARPENING YOUR AWARENESS TO THE POINT WHERE YOU CAN READ YOUR OPPONENTS' MINDS.
BUT THIS TIME YOU CHOSE THE WRONG OPPO-NENT.
UNFORTU-NATELY FOR YOU, OUR GENIUS PLAYER...
VMMMMM

...IS ABLE TO CONCEAL HIS THOUGHTS COM-PLETELY.
F&D.

WAA

GAME, OSHI-TARI! 1 GAME TO 4!

HYO-TEI!! HYO-TEI!!

AHA HA HA! THAT F&D WAS PER-FECT!

HYOTEI!! HYOTEI!!

HE'S GOOD ...

HE BROKE MOMO'S PACE EASILY.

WAAA
NOT TO MENTION HE'S GOT QUITE A POKER FACE.
...

GAK
MY FORE-HAND?!
!
DSH
15-LOVE!!

F.A.S.
...
WAA
YUSHI'S F.A.S. WON'T ...
...GIVE YOU A CHANCE TO EVEN SQUARE UP!
AA

S.S.A.S.
HE'S ON IT! THIS TIME IT'S THE S.S.A.S. !!
YUSHI OSHITARI, "THE PLAYER OF A THOUSAND TECHNIQUES," IS DOMINATING NOW!!
SEIGAKU TENNIS CLUB

IT'S IN BOUNDS ?!
GON
MO-MOMO ?!!
GAME, OSHI-TARI. 5 GAMES TO 4.
Hey, are you all right?

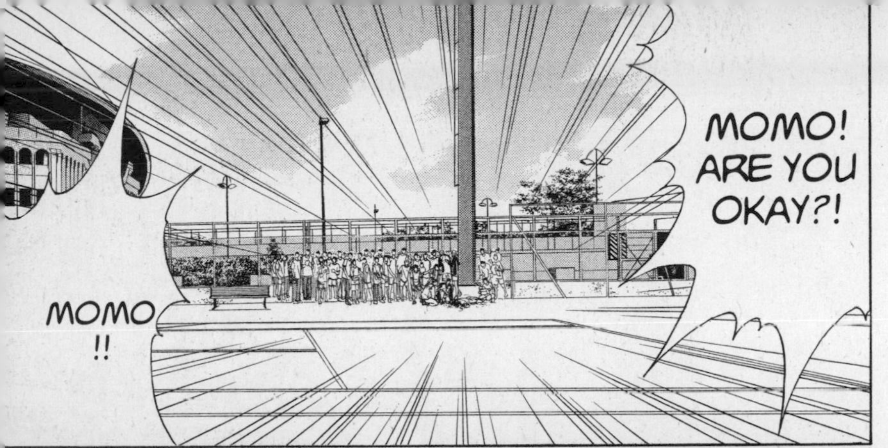
MOMO! ARE YOU OKAY?!
MOMO !!

OH, MAN... AM I... GONNA LOSE...?

CAN YOU HEAR ME, MOMO ?!
HE'S BLEED-ING!!

NO WAY... WHERE'S MY RACQUET?

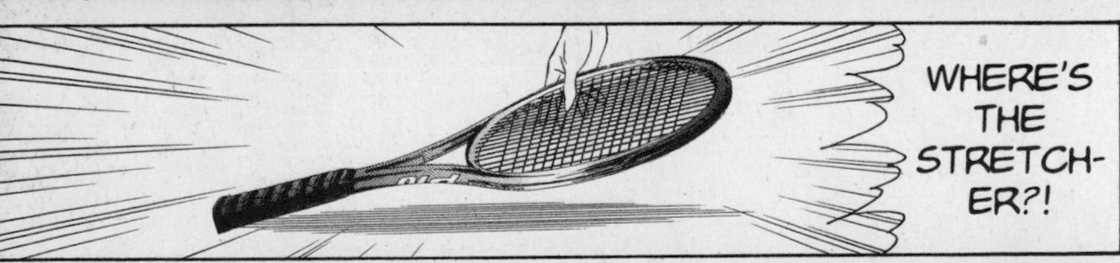
WHERE'S THE STRETCH-ER?!

I... CAN STILL...

YOU NEED TO GO CRAZIER OUT THERE, MOMO.

WHAT? YOU TRYING TO TELL ME TO BEAT HIM IN TEN MINUTES?
YUP.
YOU COULD SHOW A LITTLE CONCERN FOR ME, Y'KNOW.
ZSH...
!
HE'S GETTING BACK ON THE COURT?! IS HE INVINCIBLE OR SOME-THING?

YUSHI
...
I KNOW, KEIGO!
I KNOW TO EXPECT THE UNEXPECTED FROM THEM.

SEIGAKU
FWSSH
I'LL USE EVERY-THING I HAVE TO FINISH THIS!

LOOKS LIKE IN THE END THIS IS ALL I HAVE...
HRAAA!!
SEIGAKU

JACK-KNIFE!!
SEIGAKU
DAAAA
I SEE... A CUNNING STRATEGY.
FOOLING YOUR OPPONENT BY PLAYING AT 70% EARLY IN THE MATCH...
...SO YOU CAN MAKE YOUR GAME AT 100% SEEM EVEN MORE POWERFUL.

HE LOBBED IT BACK!
DOK
HOW-EVER ...
HUAAA!!
NO, MOMO, DON'T USE YOUR SMASH!
I'VE BEEN PLAYING AT 70% TOO!
...WHAT A COINCIDENCE.

HE WASN'T PLAYING AT 70%!
IT WAS CLOSER TO 40—NO, 30%!

KA-BOOM !!

THE 3RD CHARACTER POPULARITY POLL RESULTS!!

8TH	EIJI KIKUMARU	(4,484 VOTES)	"Woo-hoo! Thanks!"
9TH	MASAHARU NIO	(4,431 VOTES)	"Phwee ♪"
10TH	KIYOSUMI SENGOKU	(4,149 VOTES)	"Sweet ♡! Thanks, all!"
11TH	BUNTA MARUI	(3,535 VOTES)	"This ranking is proof of my genius."
12TH	RYO SHISHIDO	(3215 VOTES)	"I'll make it to the top in my own way."
13TH	JIRO AKUTAGAWA	(3,210 VOTES)	"I'm so Ha———P!!"
14TH	RENJI YANAGI	(3,165 VOTES)	"I cannot believe I placed behind Sadaharu..."
15TH	SEIICHI YUKIMURA	(3,075 VOTES)	"Well, I'll just have to advance from here."
16TH	HAJIME MIZUKI	(2,865 VOTES)	"*Eheheh...* My popularity is universal."
17TH	SHUICHIRO OISHI	(2,757 VOTES)	"What?! I finished above Momo and Kaoru?!"
18TH	KAORU KAIDO	(2,718 VOTES)	"...*hisss*..."
19TH	KOJIRO SAEKI	(2,436 VOTES)	"Don't count out Rokkaku just yet!"
20TH	CHOTARO OTORI	(2,154 VOTES)	"I did it, Ryo! I made 20th place!"

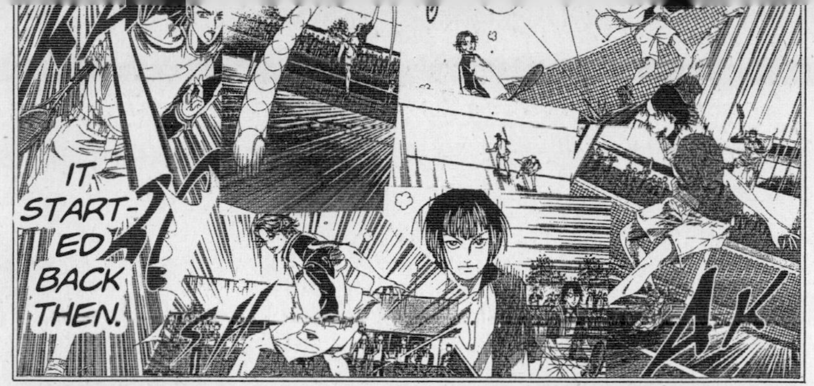

IT STARTED BACK THEN.

NOW I KNOW WHY...
...I'VE BEEN FEELING SO LOST.
SHPAA

I WON'T MAKE IT TO THE TOP...

GENIUS 277: BLOODY SHOWDOWN

... UNLESS I DEFEAT YOU HERE!
MOMO-SHIRO!
GENIUS 277:
BLOODY SHOWDOWN

THIS IS TURNING INTO AN AMAZING MATCH!

HUAAAAAA!!
KA-BOOM

MOMO'S PUSHING HIMSELF WAY TOO HARD!

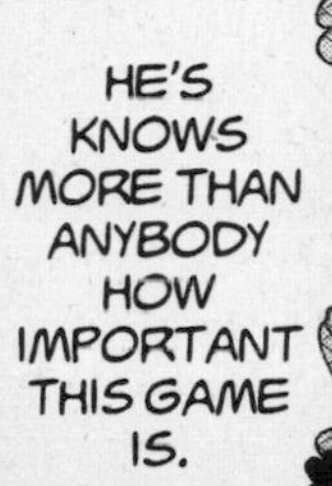
HE'S KNOWS MORE THAN ANYBODY HOW IMPORTANT THIS GAME IS.

WAA

LIKE A "VOLCANO ABOUT TO ERUPT"?

YES. THE STRONGER HIS OPPONENT IS, THE BETTER HE PLAYS.
HE'S DORMANT NOW AS HE STRIVES TO IMPROVE.
BUT HE'S GAINING EXPLOSIVE POWER.

PLAYING HIM AGAINST GOOD PLAYERS WILL HELP FURTHER HIS DEVELOPMENT EVEN—
!

HEY, CAPTAIN. PLAY AGAINST ME, WILL YA?
HYOTEI DOESN'T PLAN ON LOSING TO US TWICE.
THEY'VE THROWN AWAY ALL THEIR PRIDE...
HYO-TEI! HYO-TEI!
HYOTEI!! HYOTEI!!
...AND ALL THEIR PAST GLORY FOR THE SAKE OF REVENGE.
THAT'S WHY...

I CAN'T LOSE !!
DOOOM
FOOL.
MOMOSHIRO'S INJURY IS WORSE THAN HE THINKS. YOU KNOW THAT, DON'T YOU, YUSHI? STRETCH THIS GAME OUT!
ZSH

HAA!!

HUA!!
HYA!!
!
YUSHI... YOU...
THAT IDIOT. HE'S LETTING HIS EMOTIONS TAKE CONTROL.

SORRY, KEIGO. IT'S RARE TO FIND A PLAYER LIKE HIM.

SQK SQK

!
HE'S GET-TING EVEN STRON-GER..
SH
THOK
IS THERE NO LIMIT TO HIS POWER?!

NOT YOU...

IT HAS TO BE ME...
YUSHI ?!
KRRK...
KRRK
KRRK

YEAH!! HE KNOCKED HIS RAC-QUET OUTTA HIS—
HUFF
HUFF

SEIGAKU
TENNIS CLUB
SEIGAKU
SEIGAKU

GAME AND SET! OSHITARI WINS, 6 GAMES TO 4!
WAAAAA

THUMP
WHAT AM I SUPPOSED TO DO AGAINST SOMETHIN' LIKE THAT?

BY THE WAY ...
...YOU'RE MORE OF A HOT-HEAD THAN YOU LOOK, HUH?

YOU'RE A FOOL.
Go to the hospital.

THE 3RD CHARACTER POPULARITY POLL RESULTS!! 

21ST	JIN AKUTSU	(2,028 VOTES)
22ND	GENICHIRO SANADA	(1,974 VOTES)
23RD	HIROSHI YAGYU	(1,743 VOTES)
24TH	SAKUNO RYUZAKI	(1,584 VOTES)
25TH	TAKESHI MOMOSHIRO	(1,536 VOTES)
26TH	AKIRA KAMIO	(1,527 VOTES)
27TH	GAKUTO MUKAHI	(1,455 VOTES)
28TH	AYANA TEZUKA	(1,419 VOTES)
29TH	YOSHIRO AKAZAWA	(1,398 VOTES)
30TH	KENTARO MINAMI	(1,386 VOTES)
31ST	WAKASHI HIYOSHI	(1,359 VOTES)
32ND	KALPIN	(1,356 VOTES)
33RD	YUTA FUJI	(1,284 VOTES)
34TH	KURANOSUKE SHIRAISHI	(1,140 VOTES)
35TH	RYOGA ECHIZEN	(1,133 VOTES)
36TH	SHINJI IBU	(1,062 VOTES)
37TH	HARUKAZE KUROHANE	(987 VOTES)
38TH	TAKASHI KAWAMURA	(960 VOTES)
39TH	TARO SAKAKI	(921 VOTES)
40TH	HIKARU AMANE	(858 VOTES)
41ST	MUNEHIRO KABAJI	(831 VOTES)
41ST	SENRI CHITOSE	(831 VOTES)
43RD	KIPPEI TACHIBANA	(816 VOTES)
44TH	ATSUSHI KISARAZU	(768 VOTES)
45TH	KENYA OSHITARI	(711 VOTES)
46TH	TAKESHI KONOMI	(609 VOTES)
47TH	JACKAL KUWAHARA	(591 VOTES)
48TH	TAICHI DAN	(579 VOTES)
49TH	KINTARO TOYAMA	(567 VOTES)
50TH	RYO KISARAZU	(522 VOTES)

93,211 total votes! Ryoma's in first place once again! Sadaharu's high finish is outstanding, but he did show his butt after all [laughs]. Anyway, if we took another poll right now, the rankings would probably be different.

Thank you very much for all your votes.

GENIUS 278: SET YOUR HEART ON FIRE

MY RIGHT HAND'S STILL NUMB.
MOMO-SHIRO AND HIS STUPID RAW POWER.

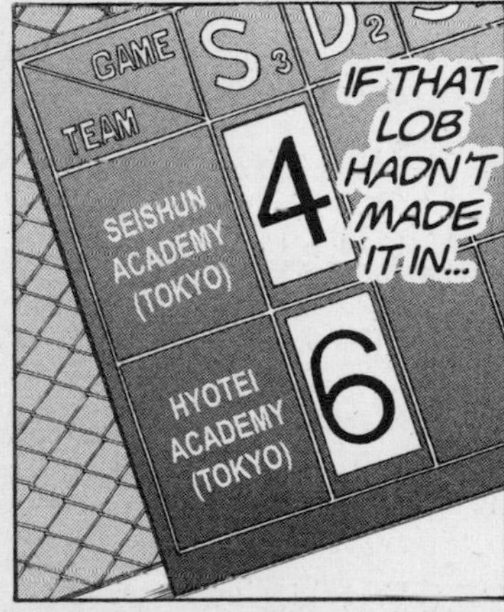

IF THAT LOB HADN'T MADE IT IN...

GENIUS 278: SET YOUR HEART ON FIRE

NO, MOMO.
YOU PLAYED A GREAT GAME.

THANKS TO YOU...

A-
A
A
A
...A CERTAIN SOMEONE'S A LITTLE FIRED UP.

I DON'T THINK ANYBODY CAN STOP HIM NOW.

YUSHI'S KIND OF A HOT-HEAD, ISN'T HE?
TUD
SHUT UP. DON'T TALK BAD ABOUT YOUR TEAM-MATES.
ZSH
AAAA
OH, WELL!!
OH I'M SOOO SORRY, GAKUTO ...
TCH. THIS IS WHY I DIDN'T WANNA PAIR UP WITH YOU.

LET'S GO!!

WAAAA
HYO-TEI!! HYO-TEI!!
HYO-TEI!! HYO-TEI!!

HEY, SADA-HARU!
WANNA KNOW THE CHANCES OF YOU GUYS LOSING?

IT'S 100%!

SEE? THEY'RE SCARED.
YOU WEREN'T SUP-POSED TO TELL THEM YET.

YOU BETTER STOP TALKIN' CRAP!
WHSH

KLANK

BETTER WATCH YOUR RACQUET.

WE'LL SHOW YOU THERE'S ALWAYS SOMEBODY BETTER.
ONE-SET MATCH! SEISHUN TO SERVE!
HYOTEI!! HYOTEI!!
HYOTEI!! HYOTEI!!
TWITCH...

!
RAA
WAKA-SHI'S STARTING WITH HIS ENBU TENNIS?! AND...
SWISH

...GAKUTO'S ALREADY USING HIS MOON-SAULT!
THEY'RE GOING ALL OUT...
HYO-TEI!! HYO-TEI!!
HYO-TEI!! HYO-TEI!!

KAORU ...
SHHF
KAORU'S GOING ALL THE WAY BACK TO THE BASE-LINE!
THAT MEANS ...!
SWA — Y
SEIGAKU
THAT'S IT, KAORU! DON'T PAY ANY ATTENTION TO 'EM!!
SWA — Y

HYO-TEI!! HYO-TEI!!
HYO-TEI!! HYO-TEI!!
HYO-TEI!! HYO-TEI!!
WHAT'S THE MATTER, SADAHARU? YOU SCARED?
WE'LL OVER-THROW YOU.
HYO-TEI!!

OM

I TOLD YOU SOMEONE'S A LITTLE FIRED UP.

テニスの王子様
THE PRINCE OF TENNIS

GENIUS 279: A QUICK MATCH
D-DID YOU SEE THAT?!
MUTTER
40-LOVE !!
IT WAS LIKE THEY WERE SWAL-LOWED UP BY A WATER-FALL...
"WATER-FALL," HUH?

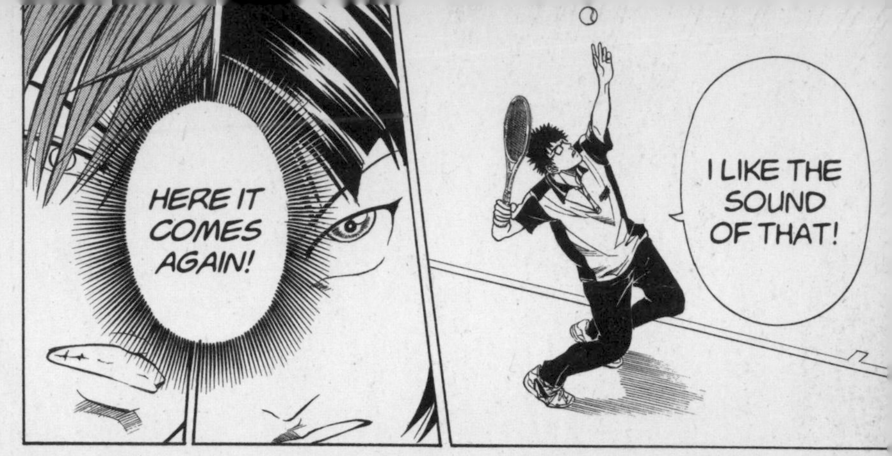

I LIKE THE SOUND OF THAT!
HERE IT COMES AGAIN!

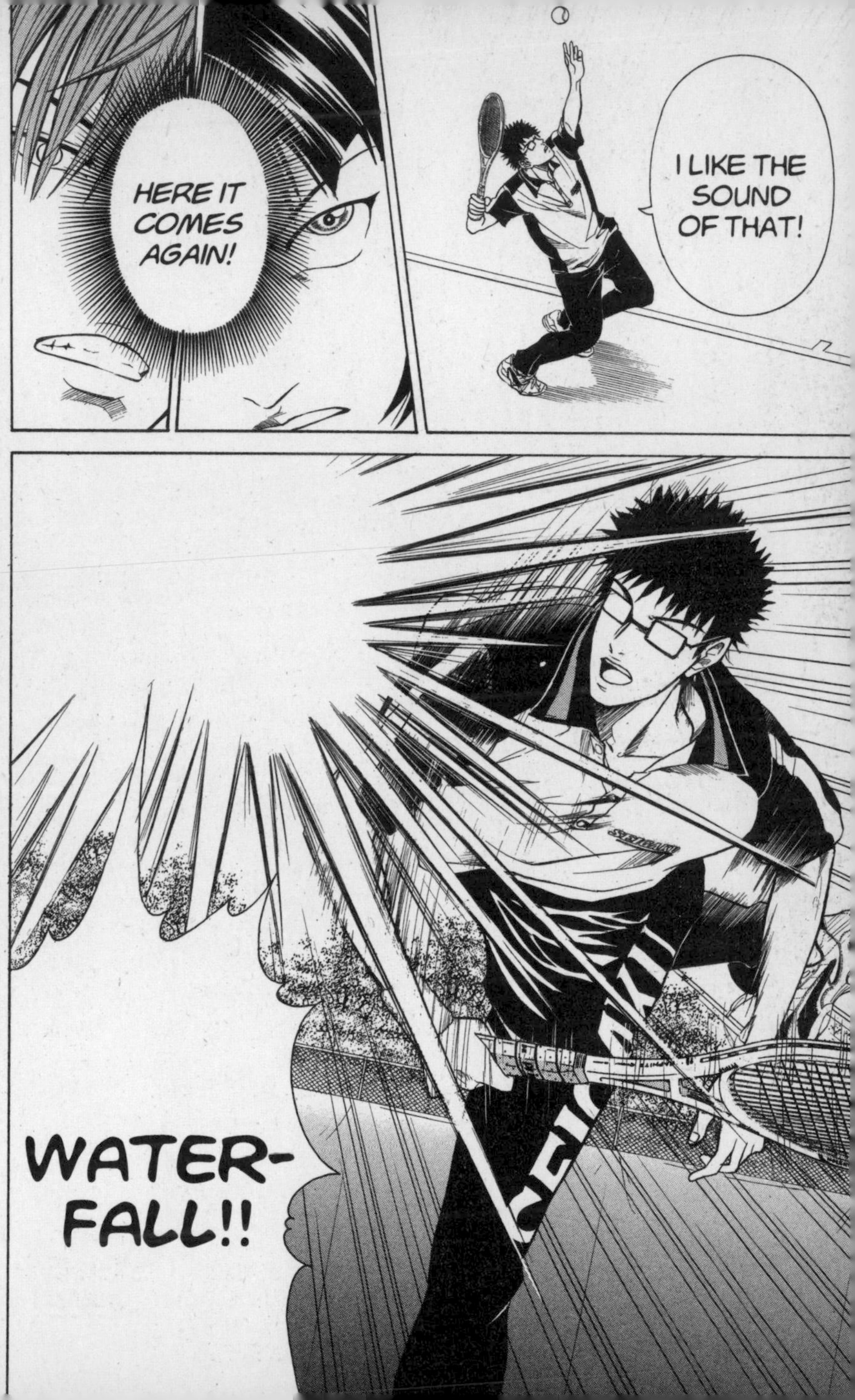

WATER-FALL!!

GAME, SEISHUN! I-LOVE!
UN-BELIEV-ABLE!
HE'S TAKEN HIS SUPER HIGH-SPEED SERVE TO ANOTHER LEVEL!

CHOTARO, IT'S ON PAR WITH YOUR SCUD SERVE.

NO, RYO... IT'S FASTER THAN MY SCUD.

SNAP
HAGINO-SUKE. HOW FAST WAS IT?

131 MPH. HOLY...

RAA
SADA-HARU!
SADA-HARU!
THAT'S 6 MPH OVER THE TOURNA-MENT RECORD.

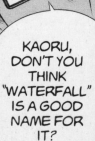

KAORU, DON'T YOU THINK "WATERFALL" IS A GOOD NAME FOR IT?

HUH? UH... SURE ...

GENIUS 279:

A QUICK MATCH

IT'S OUR TURN NOW, SEISHUN! C'MON!!
BSH
DOWN THE MIDDLE ?!
KH...
KAORU, LOOK OU–

THAT WAS TOO EASY!
15-LOVE!!

IT'S HOPE-LESS !!

GAKU-TO'S UN-STOP-PABLE!!
HYO-TEI! HYO-TEI!
HYO-TEI! HYO-TEI!
WAAA
GAME, HYOTEI! 3 GAMES TO 1!

I DON'T UNDER-STAND THIS...
ZSH
THEY'RE PUSHING THE PACE WAY TOO HARD.
SEIGAKU
20% CHANCE OF A POACH...
!
DM M
IT'S A POACH!

GASP
WOAH !!
I WON'T LET 'EM SCORE!
SWSH..
SWW
RE-VERSE SNAKE!
WM

ZSHAAAA
HAH !!

KAAAAA
LOVE-30!
WAA
LOVE-40!
WAA
HYO-TEI! HYO-TEI!
DON'T TELL ME THEY'RE ...
HYO-TEI! HYO-TEI!

AH, YES.
DO YOU THINK WE'D BE STUPID ENOUGH TO PLAY AN ENDURANCE GAME AGAINST YOU TWO?
WAAA
THE BIG-GEST ...
... THREAT TO US WOULD BE...
SEIGAKU
A QUICK MATCH !!

NO.
WE CAN'T FOLLOW THIS PACE!
CALCULATE! ANALYZE!
PLAY BASED ON DATA!
GAKUTO'S WEAKEST SPOT IN THIS SITUATION IS...
NOW! DOWN THE MIDDLE!!

GAME, HYOTEI! 5 GAMES TO 2!
OVERTHROW!!

テニスの王子様
THE PRINCE OF TENNIS

GENIUS 280: PROBABILITY... 100%

PRETTY ANTI-CLIMACTIC, HUH, GAKUTO?

LIKE WE'D GET INTO AN ENDURANCE MATCH AGAINST *THAT* PAIR. HA HA!

GAME, HYOTEI! 5 GAMES TO 2!
WAAA

GAKUTO LOST IN THE KANTO TOURNAMENT BY BEING TOO AGGRESSIVE AND RUNNING OUT OF STAMINA.
I ASSUMED THAT HE'D BE TRYING TO SAVE HIS STRENGTH IN THIS MATCH.
THAT SAKAKI... BY PAIRING GAKUTO WITH WAKASHI, WHO PLAYS A FAST GAME...
HE PLANS ON HAVING THE MATCH END BEFORE GAKUTO'S STAMINA RUNS OUT.

SEISHUN'S ONLY WON ON INUI'S SERVICE GAMES.
COACH RYUZAKI ...
THIS IS THE ORDER THAT WILL LEAD HYOTEI TO VICTORY!

ONLY ONE MORE GAME? I CAN KEEP GOING FULL-ON!
DSH
LET'S END THIS AL-READY!!
ZSH
HYO-TEI! HYO-TEI!
HYO-TEI! HYO-TEI!
RAA
AA
15-LOVE!
DMM

ALL SEI-SHUN CAN DO IS PLAY DE-FENSE!
WAAAA
GAKUTO, STAY SHARP 'TIL THE END...
THEY CAN'T STOP HYOTEI'S NO. 2 DOUBLES PAIR!
I KNOW WHAT I HAVE TO DO.
DM
SHAAA
30-LOVE!

WHEN WE FOUND OUT HYOTEI GOT INTO THE NATIONALS, NO ONE WAS HAPPIER THAN ME AND GAKUTO.
BE-CAUSE IT MEANT THAT WE COULD FINALLY OVER-THROW SEISHUN!
IT SHOULDN'T HAVE BEEN SEISHUN AT THE NATIONALS IN THE FIRST PLACE! IT SHOULD'VE BEEN HYOTEI!!

40-LOVE!!
HYOTEI ACAD-EMY MATCH POINT!
YES! IT'S FINALLY MATCH POINT!!
ONE MORE POINT! ONE MORE POINT!
ONE MORE POINT! ONE MORE POINT!
NO...
LOOK AT HOW MUCH THEY'RE SWEATING.

?
I SEE... IT APPEARED AS THOUGH THEY REACHED MATCH POINT RELATIVELY QUICKLY...

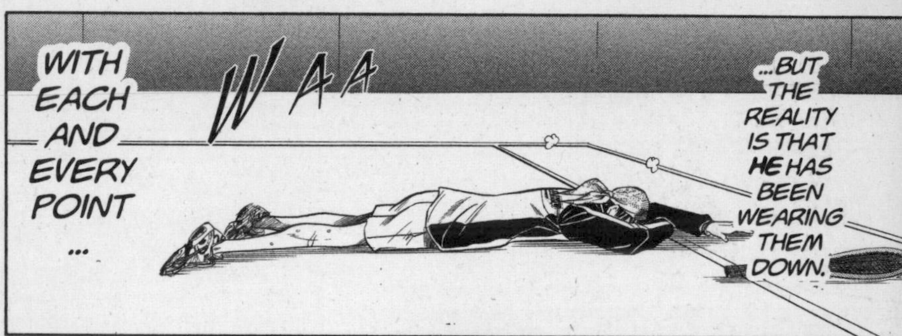

...BUT THE REALITY IS THAT HE HAS BEEN WEARING THEM DOWN.
WAA
WITH EACH AND EVERY POINT ...

...THEY FELL FURTHER INTO KAIDO'S TRAP.

ONE MORE POINT! ONE MORE POINT!
WAAAAA
ONE MORE POINT! ONE MORE POINT!
WHAT AT FIRST SEEMED LIKE A QUICK MATCH...
PAAAA
...IS ALL OF THE SUDDEN AN ENDURANCE TEST.

SEI-
SHUN!!
SEI-
SHUN!!
HYO-
TEI!!
HYO-
TEI!!
WAA
AAA
!
WHY
CAN'T
WE
SCORE
...?
WE'RE
SO
CLOSE
TO
WINNING,
BUT...
GASP
TH-
THAT'S
—?!

A DOUBLE POACH?!

THE CHANCES OF A DOUBLE POACH... 100%.
SEIGAKU
IS IT OVER ...?
HE'S USING DATA TENNIS?!
DON'T GIVE UP JUST YET...

WAKA-
SHI,
GO
FOR
IT!!
H-HE
REACHED
IT!
THE
CHANCES
OF WAKASHI
JUMPING AND
REACHING IT...
100%

AND THE CHANCES OF KAORU'S NEW TECHNIQUE...
SHWM

TENNIS CLUB
..."THE "TORNADO SNAKE," SCORING ...

...100%.

TO...
TOR-NADO SNAKE?! KAORU'S GOT A NEW SHOT!!
40-15!
HEY.
THERE'S MORE WHERE THAT CAME FROM.

THE TWO HYOTEI PLAYERS WHO GAVE EVERY-THING THEY HAD TO WIN...
GAME AND SET! SEISHUN WINS, 7 GAMES TO 5!

...NO LONGER HAD THE STAMINA TO CONTINUE PLAYING.
WE DID IT!!

テニスの王子様
THE PRINCE OF TENNIS

GENIUS 281: UNDEFEATABLE

SEISHUN ACADEMY (TOKYO)
47
HYOTEI ACADEMY
65
NO. 3 SINGLES, MOMOSHIRO VS. OSHITARI, ENDED WITH HYOTEI'S VICTORY.
THEN INUI AND KAIDO CAME FROM BEHIND TO BEAT MUKAHI AND HIYOSHI IN NO. 2 DOUBLES.

NOW THE SCORE IS TIED AT 1 ALL...

THE NO. 2 SINGLES MATCH WILL NOW BEGIN!

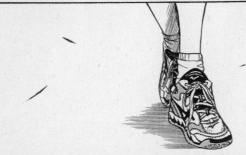

SEIGAKU
SEIGAKU
SEIGAKU
SEIGAKU
GENIUS 281:
UNDEFEATABLE

SEIGAKU
SEIGAKU

WHAT ?!
SEIGAKU

WAA
TEZU-KA'S PLAYING IN NO. 2 SINGLES ?!
WHAT THE HECK IS GOING ON?

WAA

AGAINST KABAJI? *HEH HEH HEH.* THIS ONE'S IN THE BAG!♪

LET'S HAVE A GOOD MATCH.

...

ONE-SET MATCH! TEZUKA TO SERVE !!
KUNIMITSU, I KNEW YOU'D PLAY IN NO. 2 SINGLES...

HAAH!!

...AND NOW YOU'RE IN FOR A SUR-PRISE.
WOAH! THIS IS A CRAZY RALLY!
HUA !!
SH

RAAAA
KABAJI'S HOLDING UP AGAINST KUNI-MITSU!
WAAA
WHAT IS KUNIMITSU DOING?
HE HAD A CHANCE TO SCORE USING HIS ZERO-SHIKI DROP SHOT.

HAH !!
WAAAH
THOK
THOK
HRAH !!

HE DIDN'T DECIDE *NOT* TO USE THE ZERO-SHIKI!
HE *CAN'T* USE IT! KABAJI CAN MIMIC HIS OPPONENT'S SHOTS JUST BY SEEING THEM ONCE!
SHU-SUKE'S RIGHT.
HE'S RETURNING KUNIMITSU'S SHOTS EXACTLY AS THEY'RE HIT TO HIM.
JUST LIKE HE DID WITH TAKA'S HADOKYU.

?
ZSH...
ZSSH...
LOOK! KUNI-MITSU HASN'T ...
...MOVED EVEN A STEP FROM THE SAME SPOT!

IT'S THE
TEZUKA
ZONE!!

EVERY BALL KUNI-MITSU HITS...
RETURNS AS IF IT'S BEING DRAWN BACK TOWARD HIM.
THE TEZUKA ZONE... ONLY KUNIMITSU COULD PULL OFF SOME-THING LIKE THAT.

K-Kabaji
Zone?!

YOU FELL RIGHT FOR IT, KUNIMITSU. AND NOW HYOTEI WILL WIN!

テニスの王子様
THE PRINCE OF TENNIS

GENIUS 282:
KUNIMITSU IN CRISIS

VWOOM
HE'S MIMICK-ING EVEN THE TEZUKA ZONE?!
N-NO WAY...

READ
THIS
WAY

BE-
CAUSE
KABAJI
IS SO
PURE...
HE'S ABLE
TO ABSORB AN
OPPONENT'S
TECHNIQUE
JUST BY SEEING
IT ONCE.
WAA
TO KABAJI,
IT DOESN'T
MATTER HOW
GOOD OR BAD
HIS OPPONENT
IS.

IN FACT,
THE
STRON-
GER
THEY
ARE...
BAAA
...THE
BETTER
IT IS FOR
HYOTEI!

SHF

HAVE FUN
PLAYING
AGAINST
YOUR-
SELF...
KUNI-
MITSU.

HYO-TEI!! HYO-TEI!!
HYO-TEI!! HYO-TEI!!

HYOTEI! HYOTEI !!

IT'D BE WISE NOT TO REVEAL MORE TECH-NIQUES.
IT'LL ONLY MAKE HIM STRON-GER.
KABAJI'S ABSORBING EVERY SHOT!
!
A TRAP THIS LATE IN THE ROUND...
MAYBE WE UNDER-ESTIMATED KABAJI'S POTENTIAL.
SHAAAAA

SHRAAA

ARRIVALS
Exit
4
4

CLINICAL DEPARTMENT
SURGERY/NEUROSURGERY/NEUROLOGY
OUTPATIENT CLINIC PAIN CLINIC
HOURS 9:00AM ~ 5:00PM
CLOSED SAT. AFTERNOON, SUN., HOLIDAYS
SEISHUN ACADEMY SURGICAL
SEISHUN ACADEMY SURGICAL CENTER

SEISHUN ACADEMY SURGICAL CENTER
CLINICAL DEPARTMENT
SURGERY/NEUROSURGERY/NEUROLOGY
OUTPATIENT CLINIC PAIN CLINIC
HOURS 9:00AM - 5:00PM
CLOSED SAT. AFTERNOON, SUN., HOLIDAYS
SEISHUN ACADEMY SURGICAL
FOUNDATION

WILL I... WILL I RE-COVER IN TIME ...?
POK
GRIP

HEY !!
PUT THAT DOWN, YOU RAC-QUET THIEF!
GIVE IT BACK! GIVE IT BACK! GIVE IT BACK! GIVE IT BACK! GIVE IT BACK! GIVE IT BACK! GIVE IT BACK! GIVE IT BACK! GIVE IT BACK! GIVE IT BACK!!
AH... SORRY ...

HUH. YOU'RE PRETTY OBEDI- ENT.
BUT BOY, YOU'RE BAD AT TENNIS, MR. RACQUET THIEF.
Thief?
Beginner, ain't ya?
YOU HAVE TO LIFT YOUR SHOULDER A LITTLE MORE...
WAIT, STOP. STOP IT!
NGH!
WHOA-!
THUD
OW! WHAT WAS THAT FOR?!

THAT'S NO WAY TO TREAT A LADY! APOLOGIZE!

TO BE CONTINUED IN VOL. 33!

In the Next Volume...

Kunimitsu in Kyushu

The National Tournament quarterfinals against Hyotei continue with Kunimitsu facing power player Munehiro Kabaji. During the match Seishun's captain flashes back to his time in Kyushu and the road that led him to the Nationals. Later, it's a battle of the Golden Pairs: Ryo Shishido and Chotaro Ohtori versus Shuichiro and Eiji.

Available September 2009!